LETTERS TO THE QUICK

LETTERS TO THE DEAD

WITH SELECTIONS FROM BURNSITE AND FAMILY & OTHER STRANGERS

SHIRLEY GRAVES COCHRANE

SIGNAL BOOKS CHAPEL HILL, NC

Library of Congress Cataloging-in-Publication Data

Cochrane, Shirley, 1925-

    Letters to the quick, letters to the dead : with selections from

    Burnsite and family and other strangers / Shirley Graves Cochrane.

       p.   cm.

    ISBN 0-930095-33-2 (pbk.)

    I. Title.

PS3553.027L4   1998

811'.54—dc21   98-17252

                                                               CIP

original cover design by Adele Robey

    of Phoenix Graphics, Washington, DC

design production by Cassio Lynm

author photograph by Gerry Gleason

Printed in the United States of America

To the Memory of My Father and Mother

What will they say of you, my book:
there in the market place collecting
dust, filed under the wrong letter
where you cannot be found
when my mother's ghost
comes to ask for you, claiming
this book has been praised
by wise persons, especially
one fair man travelling
from sunset into morning?

Acknowledgments

LETTERS TO THE QUICK, LETTERS TO THE DEAD

Some of the poems in *Letters to the Quick, Letters to the Dead* have appeared in the following publications: *Baltimore Review, Colorado Review, Potomac Review, Sulphur River Review, North Carolina Arts Journal, Poet Lore, Poets On, Passages North, Slow Dancer,* and *Crucible;* and the following anthologies: *Hunger* (published by Washington Writers' Publishing House), *80 on the 80's (Ashland University Poetry Press) Here's to the Land* (N.C. Poetry Society anthology), and *The Cooke Book: a Seasoning of Poets* (anthology, SCOP Publications).

FAMILY & OTHER STRANGERS ... *selections*

Family & Other Strangers was published by the Word Works, Inc., Washington, DC, 1986. Cover design by Janice Olson. Foreword by Robert Sargent. Dedication to Peter Petcoff and the Capitol Hill Poetry Group.

Some of the poems reproduced here first appeared in the following publications: *Belles Lettres; Crucible; Davidson Miscellany;* ; *Hollins Critic; International Poetry Review; Phoebe, Sibyl-Child*; and *Sulphur River Review;* and the following anthologies: *American Classic: Car Poems for Collectors* (SCOP Publications, Inc.), *Ear's Chamber* (SCOP Publications, Inc.), *Other Side of the Hill* (Capitol Hill Poetry Group).

BURNSITE ... *selections*

Burnsite was published by Washington Writers' Publishing House, Washington, DC, 1972. Graphic design and production by Copesthetic. Cover design by William Daniel Cochrane. Dedication to MWG (my mother).

Some of the poems reproduced here first appeared in the following publications: *Blue Ridge Review; DeKalb Literary Arts Journal; Hollins Critic; International Poetry Review; Ohio Journal; Phoebe; Poet Lore; Proteus; Southern Poetry Review; Uwharrie Review*; and the following anthologies: *City Celebration, 1976* (Martin Luther King Public Library); *Rye Bread: Women Poets Rising* (SCOP Publications, 1977); *The Poet Upstairs* (Washington Writers' Publishing House, 1979); and *Yearbook of American Poetry, 1980.*

LETTERS TO THE QUICK

LETTERS TO THE DEAD

THE QUICK AND THE DEAD

For a while they stay with us,
our dead, allowing us to set
a place for them at the table,
waking us
        in morning light
tolerating our tearfalls...
the dead are often merciful.

When we speak their names
they convey, by means we
do not understand, messages
such as *I am here*, and though
these could well be echoes
from our own minds
        they let us
soldier on, as one soul
advised me this very morning.

So we obey their gentle orders
and feel them move away. And who
can blame them?

Time passes
and we realize first with horror
then sadness that we cannot take
them back, whether they return
rollicking or wreathed
in elder-Hamlet gloom.

And even though
the new life, land-filled over
the old, is less than what we
had before — still, we cannot
make room for them.

Nor can they,
both the old dears and the young
taken in their prime, find in us
the beings we once were — even
our voices, let alone faces, are
those of strangers, yet strangers
who remember their good company.

Contents

Part II: The Quick

FAMILY & OTHER STRANGERS ... selections

BURNSITE ... selections

LETTERS TO THE QUICK

LETTERS TO THE DEAD

Part I: The Dead

THE GRANDMOTHER

If she ever missed the home-place
boxwoods, or longed to plant
a nail to turn the hydrangea pink;
if she thought of painting lattice-work
or the newel post shaped to bigger hands
than her own small one, or remembered
the swing hitched high in winter
clear up to the porch ceiling; if mint
beds crossed her mind, or rampant
squash vines, or her husband's orchards
bearing fruit only for bird flocks now;
if she listened for Doe Creek music
in all the lesser houses she inhabited —
if in short she mourned the world
she left when husband and son
were taken in the same hard year,
she never let on and in fact prided
herself that like a wren she could
always build a nest in any handy
    jar or hat.

THE CANDY QUEEN

The fires under her black
pots burned out fifty years
ago, but I keep the red scale
with its four black weights
and her lollipop molds that hold
the odors of pineapple and cherry
butterscotch and raspberry
in shapes of running rabbit,
pony and fiddle, cornucopia
   and Kewpie doll.

A recent dream — she
is living in a tall-standing,
burnt-sienna house, unlike
anything she ever inhabited.
She sits in an inglenook
with sister candy queens
and their teacher, Mrs. Hannah
of the Candy Institute.
Mrs. Hannah who warned,
Never wax your chocolates
and extracted promises
from her pupils to choose
only one person to share
   their secrets.

I was my grandmother's chosen
apprentice — one who rarely

washed to the elbows; raider
of showcases, sneak thief
of marzipan and nougat —
one whose fingers tangled
the glassine bags, let slip
the aridor jar, scattered
the chocolate shot, rolled
the Roman punches round
not oblong; put pecans
on top of yellow bonbons,
almond slivers on mocha creams.
And now in this dream
I come bearing a box
of miniature chocolates
waxed and shining, unworthy
    gift for a queen.

I lay the box in her lap
as the candy queens avert
their eyes and Mrs. Hannah
shudders. Pensively
my grandmother gazes
at the candy. In the days
of my failed bonbon dipping
she would say, "Never mind —
your talents lie elsewhere"
    stressing elsewhere.

5

And she always forgave me
my candy thieving, for she
too had the "sugar hunger"
and used to say, "If I'd been
a man, I'd have been a drinker."

But back to the dream —
I bid her good-bye, then turn
at the door, wondering if she
will cry me back as she used
to do in her last old days
 but she waves me on.

Out the door and down the street
(and where will I ever find
that street, that house again?)
I think of the gift I should
have brought — a loaf of Irish
bread made by her hand-written
recipe, to show her that her yeast
keeps rising, ever rising
 in this grandchild.

RELINQUISHING THE DEAD

The day after her last son's burial
my grandmother stood all morning
at the window, her reflection
mourning in the rain-mottled glass.
She had schooled herself not to weep
after the first son's death, for what
was there left worthy of her tears
till now? "Will you come to lunch?"
I asked, touching her lightly.

"Not yet," she said.
How could she sit in yellow-
napkined comfort while *he...*
although the undertaker said
these boxes are so tight
no water can ever seep in...
still, she had to keep a vigil
till the rain wept itself out
and the sun reclaimed the earth.

NANDINA

The nandina burst into bridal flowers
soon after I clipped the old berries
from last year's blossoming. Bare
branches, leafing out, berry-birthing,
flowering, bare branches again. Seasons
grab their time, then exit quietly.

And suddenly there's the ghost of my
great-grandmother sitting in her rocker
I painted fresh white last week. Nine
children she rocked (one lost — in her
day a woman was lucky to mourn just one).

She is crochetting each descendant
a bedspread: the sixteen grandchildren
the fourteen great-grands, of which I
was proud eldest...She bends
toward the light, her serene face
shadowed briefly by a grieving cloud.

So many to make up the one loss —
yet to the end she kept in her work
basket a picture of a girl wearing
Scotch bonnet and tartan, *Our Jess*
elegantly scripted on the back.

GESUNDHEIT

The pepper sneezes of my Uncle George
left cracks in the foundation
while Granny sneezed in shocked dismay
retreating from the kitchen.

My mother sneezed as though her soul
might leave her lovely body
the devil and she were having it out
with him the likely winner.

She fled the parlor with *bless-you's*
bestowed by Great Granny
who in turn sneezed out apologies
excuse it, excuse it, excuse it...

Back then I practiced kitten sneezes
light as dandelion spore
but lone survivor of us all, I now
explode like Uncle George

into *hit-cha, hit-cha, hit-cha*
and sneeze thrice for matriarchy
to scatter out their separate souls
then bless them back inside me.

9

WIDOW IN MORNING LIGHT

— for Mary

They have all left now —
daughters, sisters-in-law,
friends who stayed over.
Flowers wilt in closed-off rooms
neighbors' untouched offerings
and his spectacles where he left
them on the kitchen table.
She does not move them, nor
his bathrobe hanging on its
hook; his hair brushes she
leaves on the dresser untouched.

She does not need to fold
the newspaper back for him
today, but she does it anyway
and waits for his morning step
on the stairs, signal to start
breakfast. She makes lists
to buy oatmeal and the ginger cakes
he favored...so little laundry now
it seems hardly worth the doing...

Strange to sit in this emptiness,
the lines, "cry of absence, absence
in the heart" thrumming in her head.
Fifty-three years ... arguments
at times fierce but never quarrels

and his puns, her favorite: "Owed
on a Grecian Earn" when he mailed
his income tax check from Athens.

The incomparable companionship —
what she had missed most when he
fell silent after the first stroke
and now this more enduring silence.
Her older daughter says, *You are free
now...travel, see friends, go out,
get back your life*, and she will,
she will, but right now, she must
sit and knit together her past.

They dressed him in his Navy blues
and ribbons, and in the land-locked
chapel rising safe among its tombstones the naval hymn, "for those
in peril on the sea" was sung.
After the cremation, the younger
daughter took ashes to the sound
where he had spent his boyhood
summers, and though the widow did not
make that journey herself, she sees
in her mind's eye their fair child,
his "ewe lamb," her long hair whipping
in the wind as she relinquishes
her father's remains to the sea.

GENETIC RECKONINGS

I have my grandmother's
marbled feet — the bunions,
the hammer toes — and on
index fingers her arthritic
knobs; also her hand veins
like blue highways on old
maps, the leaf rake of bones
rising higher each year.

Her gold wedding band
adorns my right ring finger.
Riding in a cab to a party
I watch her cloned hand
pat the reticule she left
me — the same rhythm she used
when comforting this grandchild.

DANCING AT THE SAFEWAY

(a dream)

Jesters come in cap and bells
to tell me my father and mother
are to dance at the Safeway.
Come, come! they gesture.
I have never seen my father —
his death collided with my birth.
What will he make of me
               this man
who could not stay to see me?

The jesters' million tiny bells
speak as stars might; we wind
down streets until we reach
the square where Safeway's
sign lights up a dance floor,
a curtain pulled around it to hide
cat food and bathroom cleaners.

These dance partners — how will
they look? The two parted
ones, separated for half
a century? Elegant younger
man mated to the silver
beauty that she became.
And here they come!

13

I cannot greet them —
the strange etiquette of dreams —
yet they know I'm here,
their long-grown child.
                    He moves
judiciously, as though he'd just
read a book showing foot prints
prancing across the pages —
dance numbers he's trying out.
She has her girlish movements,
the quick-steps of youth.

When the dance is over,
my father draws back the curtain
and looks at Safeway offerings —
Catawba grape juice disguised
                    as champagne

frozen foods, instant puddings....
Where is the Nucco — blocks of white
margarine with their celluloids
of orange coloring? The junkets,
rennets, honest make-from-scratch
flours? This array of new products
                    confounds him.

He holds up objects: This? this?
My mother shrugs or shakes her head
or else extends a languid
arm toward the cart. The cart!
A new toy — he shifts
the kiddy seat, tests it,
the way he tested the buggy
they bought for my coming.
I want to go to him, this father,
but my mother signals:

               You must wait

And now the jesters return
to fetch me home. *Come, come,*
they beckon and deliver me
to my bed. All the rest
of that long night, movies
of my father play out
upon the screen of my shut eyes.
He rests his hand upon my mother's
acorn belly, and I, awaiting
birth, feel its weight.

AFTER THE HURRICANE

Two decades ago fire devoured
our small house and singed
the dogwoods to their roots
leaving the chimney as marker.

A house of modest pleasures
and rattling windows, burning
logs and swords above the mantel,
the generous screened-in porch...

The house that took its place
lacked its funky charm — we never
hung our hearts on its latch-string
but still, it was a place to come.

Now with bashed-in roof, the house
is not what we mourn — rather,
the land; bones of white pine, oak,
beech tangled in aromatic massacre.

We cannot resurrect our old world
a second time and make it hum.
All the young dreams must go —
the field of wild flowers cascading

to the creek, the tower overlooking
the ancient Triassic sea-bed...
Accept the inevitable —
sell out is what we must do.

Nothing compared to the loss
of a child — more like a limb
amputated or the pain of putting
a well-loved animal to sleep.

READING ROBERT FROST

— for Caroline

So here I am in your old house, climbing
toward your girlhood room, when your daughter
hands me your father's book of Frost
and says "Death of the Hired Man"
was your favorite poem in all the world.
Close as we were, I never knew you
had this bond with Frost. We talked
poetry only to complain of teachers
who tried to stuff it down our throats.

Our conversations centered on menstrual
blood and treacheries of boys, how
even when they were mean as snakes
you needed them to get to dances.
Later we talked weddings and babies —
how to have them, how not to. Later
still, formulas and recipes, gossip
of lost towns. But for us to sit down
and read "Death of the Hired Man"
would have violated the code of irony
we aspired to. So now I'll have a go
at it alone, in delayed memoriam.

First, the book's inscription
in Frost's wavering but determined
hand, then your father's answer —

two Roberts conversing on a flyleaf.
Frost ends his long note: "I just don't
like a man who doesn't like Wordsworth."
And I think of your father, a Wordsworth
man if ever I knew one, think of him
after your brother and mother and you
were all gone, how he read "Tintern Abbey"
aloud to drown out tiresome caretaker talk
his voice rising to transcendental heights.

And now I read the words I did not know
you loved, get lost in the narration —
the haymaking, the man who had nothing
to look back upon with pride or forward
to with hope. Wrapped as I am in the
moon's patternings, the hands of the kindly
woman, I forget you until the last line
leaps out: *Dead, was all he answered.*
The same answer I got when I arrived
too late for anything except to hear
the preacher sound your name and watch
your ashes being scattered among roses.

COUNTRY BURIAL

Past the yes-we-got kerosene stores
past the RR sign hung with honeysuckle
the cortege winds to the cemetery
FUNERAL markers clamped
to every hood. Slammed dead —
those words come to me
and I wonder what she thought
as that no-good car she was
going to turn in next week
stopped dead and the monster
truck barreled across
the bridge behind her.

The picture made the back pages,
before you got to the obituaries.
I think of her fine bones
and those almost too-blue
eyes and the tilt of chin —
What in God's name have they put
in that coffin?

At the cemetery her tall son
and her daughter, more beautiful
than she was, both wear black —
honest mourning clothes. The girl
leans on her stronger brother.
Their grandmother, held up by sons,
creeps to the graveside — why did she

20

live on past last year's stroke
only to be put through this?

And I remember my own mother, gone
these six years now, spared the sight
of one more younger friend carried
to a flowered grave. And there
in my attic sits the love seat
Mama left her, the thing I never
managed to get downstairs, thinking
there would always be time.

AWAITING MIDNIGHT

The dogs have barked the moon up high
The stars have lulled the dogs to sleep
A mist scuds across the pond
Mourning doves and water fowl
await the morning

Now is the ghost-walker time
So come, old love, slightly scary
in your silvered body
Here — sit beside me on this bench
and let me hear your voice
study your transfigured face
to see if I still know you

NEIGHBORHOOD

It has come again —
the widow stands at her window:
How could he leave me in winter?
The comforts of drawn curtains,
tea, lit fire all beckon, but first
this last light-hour must be endured.

We cry our *why's* into the wind, wonder
how we can spare another. Yesterday
we went the old trail delivering
death notes — two gone now,
two bone brothers; and who left
to whistle us up each morning?

And which of us will follow after?
our names left trembling in doorways
we were meant to enter, our letters
still coming to the proper boxes —
You are there, we address you
We will not take death for an answer.

DEVELOPMENT

Without the trees, houses meant
to be shadowed are strobe-lighted,
the mad professor's cabin open
to gunfire. Yet they've kept
the lay of land, this new asphalt
laid on the old trail's roadbed.
Uphill stands the brown bungalow
where I was born; the sun full
upon it strips away protective
coloration, transforms it into
shy animal caught in crosshairs.

Below it, like a beached ark,
rides the house my father built.
From the prow of my room, a look-
out over forests, I used to hear
the woods-beast panting; not a
soothing sound but one I grew
accustomed to. Should I return
to live out my lost life there,
I would hear the slowed pulse
of that endangered species
        still beating.

THE TRANSMUTATION OF DWELLINGS

In Ireland you find them —
houses taken back by land,
trees grown from their thatch.
Vines take over the work of nails
and keep windows from chattering
like arthritic grannies.

And here too, off old 86, you see
houses — honeysuckled, nested
with wrens — where meat cleavers
still hang on hooks, curtain scraps
persist on rods, greened Sunday
suits swing from light fixtures.

The air is heavy with mice
and the musk of the cats
they've survived. You can
find play-pretties of doomed
children and crazed mirrors
into which the sun glances.

The remnants of these lived
lives bring on a melancholy
as when an unknown kinsman
dies and you are summoned
to the burial — come and gone
before you ever knew he'd lived.

IN THE BISHOP'S GARDEN

It is much the same as when
they used to come in his last
diminished days — bees
working a patch of lamb's ear,
rue and phlox and bleeding heart,
foxgloves with their wallpapered insides;
Van Gogh splashes and roses of every color...

Faint outlines of bone show
through the granite garments
of the Prodigal and his father.
Someone has placed a lavender rose
on the young man's bent knee.
The father clutches his son's head —
the way she'd longed to hold *him*
against his inevitable leave-taking.
Whenever he would tire
they used to go to the gazebo.
She tries three paths.
You can get lost in this maze —
he was the one who could always find
the way, as though he held
an invisible lead-string.

Everywhere there are memorial benches —
To the Memory of...To the *Beloved*
Memory is what she'll have engraved
on the one she means to order.
Some plaques give not names
but titles: spouse, friend...
How will she describe herself
in bronze — she, more than lover
less than wife? one whose loss
still knocks against the Adam-rib.

LOVERS IN WINTER

When summer's ground freezes
and signs warn
of bridges iced over
wherever will spring's
young lovers go?

Adulterers brave snow storms
to seek one more motel night
as the safe-marrieds
their furnaces roared out
stretch on pallets
before open fires
and have an evening
of unexpected love.

While in the graveyard
marked by marble headboards
the wraiths of old-timey lovers
(properly married, long buried)
grope through frozen roots
to touch each others' bones.

FINAL DWELLING PLACE

Riding the Carolinian
DC to NC, I'm fooled
every time by that same
miniature mansion
with two marble columns.

That's where I'll move —
compress possessions
to fit the space
enough for a cat,
some books... all
I'll need in old age.

Then I notice the neighboring
tombstones and sigh an *Oh!*
of recognition — this is
a vault, family tomb.

Happened again just yesterday —
my chosen house flashed by
the train window.
Can't get a lease —
permanently occupied.

Still, if it were mine
I'd put hydrangeas
in those planters
beside the columns,
have a brick path...

OLD TRAINS

All night they thread our sleep;
their harmonica chords express
us back to the country of longing.
Like locomotives in sepia photographs
they return us to childhood meadows,
with the quick leap of setting out,
the slow groan of return. But beware
of their tempo; do not lean toward
their destination. They run backward,
backward in time, to pick up people
waiting at forgotten stations. Remember —
it is a while before we have to board.

LETTERS TO THE QUICK

LETTERS TO THE DEAD

Part II: The Quick

TRACKS

In the countryside the engine's mourning
wail floats like a scarf; never stilled,
it seems to catch in the wheels and vibrate
there above the rocking beat that is the train's
    own language.

Then in the station its muted cry gives way
to full-throated scream, and those debarking
and arriving feel the steel power
of this locomotive god in the stomach
    and solar plexus.

Small towns, asleep for decades, empty out
their citizens at this moment, and men
who faintly remember Teddy Roosevelt
flashing his Bull Moose teeth from the
    observation car

crutch their bones down to the depot
and give a feeble wave as the monster
starts up again, wailing through small-
town dawns, hurtling on to its next
    destination.

LONG TIME PASSING

— for my sons

Of all remembered journeys, the one
that travels best from then to now
is this: Dan, fresh from Apple Farm
teaching us his new-learned song,
"Where Did All the Flowers Go?"
as we rode south toward home singing —
Dan's steady tenor, my faltering alto,
Tom's basso profondo — long time passing

swiftly over the toll roads, past ruined
landscapes of cheap motels, cement toads,
bathtub pools. Adoptable dogs pled
with us under the sign of Stuckey.
Then the journey resumed — the flower
query, the whereabouts of soldiers,
the mother-spin of fear — were these
boys singing their own dirge?

I wish I had foreseen the smaller
deaths — life's totals, tolls taken —
instead of staring mutely at the one skulled grin.
For though sons survive, there is the *just
barely*...Back then I knew none of this,
nor did they. I named my fear *neurosis*
and we rode on singing as though home
would wait forever in that same sweet space.

34

THRUST

Think of the room, the lost girl
think of the emptied houses
of your life. Remember how thunder
came to break the back of August
the sky opening in jags?
Remember October's saffron
afternoons? Look at the distant
picture through the bottom
of your glass — a miniature
world you cannot enter.

Think of your grandmother's
fisted pride — hand clenched
not in anger but resolve.
Then move on — move on
as though you were wearing
her black galoshes, unbuckled,
stomping, stomping. Judgment
day must not find you
rooted to the earth.

CHANGES

Nothing does she throw away
grudges every change of wind
each new slicing of the moon.
Yet she lost the lock
of her father's hair
upon an unnamed street
and just last night she took
into her widow's bed
another lover.

GETTING THERE OURSELVES

Our fathers have been gone so long we've almost
forgotten how they looked in double-breasted
pin-striped suits, how their eyes shone
behind rainbow-rimmed glasses. Sometimes
we can recapture their morning struts,
their homecomings to bourbon and branch water.

We see our mothers in their morning-glory aprons
bending to take lemon spongettes from 1930's ovens;
in our minds, that is — actually only one is left
and she doing poorly in the nursing home built
where the Weaver's cows used to graze, relinquishing
their mortgaged milk for our tables.

We think of ourselves as the young crowd
even as we board the train for classmates'
funerals (a third one buried last week).
What's happened is that still in our youthful
regalia we've been tapped for the older
generation — an honor we never wanted.

THE OLD GIRLS

So here we are again
not the same of course
and certainly not better
    than ever
but *here* — do remember
we are here.

One of us has lost
    a leg
another, a mind
but got it back again
two have lost breasts
several, husbands
to younger women
or to the grave —
passed, deceased, *gone* —
I myself prefer plain *dead* —
husbands perfected
by that finality, death.

And of course some of us
have lost our lives as well
and lie beside those husbands
in the restored cemetery
where we the quick
will journey after lunch

carrying herbal wreaths
to perfume the ground
above their heads

But first, but first
the excellent lunch
made from recipes
handed down from grandmothers
     and great-aunts
And wine! We will have wine
two glasses apiece perhaps.

So let us dine before
we set off to visit
our fallen comrades
steadying ourselves
on our foolish heels
resting from time to time
on the steadfast stone wall
like us, surviving.

THREE WOMEN SWIMMING A RIVER

Only the ghosts of jelly fish remain
forming like semen for next year's assault.
A large school of spot make a **V**
just under the water, turning sideways
to flash their silver knives. "Schooling
fish are not biting fish," one of our husbands
once said.

And which of us, we ask ourselves
as we walk into water, putting
feet carefully onto what feels
like a long-submerged water buffalo —
which of us ever got enough
of any man's wisdom before he
took off to be buried, or married
to someone else?

Which man ever proved he would not
be bled to death by mosquitoes?
Or told us why there are ribbons
of dark and light, cold and sun
in this water?

They left before we learned
that the fine sand ringing
the far bank is really broken
shells and bottles like ones
we cut our feet on at home
dock, or that water, pure blue
at the horizon line, is brown
as water we've left behind, now
transformed from this distance
into flawless blue.

CENTURY MARK

I've waited too late —
should have come last year, before you went to bed.
You refuse to see me and who can blame you —
we've not laid hand on hand for ten long years.

You were ninety then —
building your iris garden. One species resembled
a bat, another a sleep-mouse, and there was a pure
black one called — for aesthetics, I suppose — *purple.*
This year three stout oaklets rise from your shingles
and Virginia creeper obliterates the windows.

Folly doesn't paw out
to greet me, and I hear her obituary from Emily.
Two lean rippers have replaced her and made threads
of the best chair ("Cats are my folly" illustrated again).

Anyway, like it or not,
here I am with a basket of dried chrysanthemums
to which all the flower ladies contributed
and gave their best basket. They no longer sit
beneath the Bank's mulberry (dead as Folly,
both Bank and tree). Instead they form a line
in the mall's promenade, which helps me see
why you refuse to go down town anymore.

Emily sets the basket
on the piano beneath *The Peaceable Kingdom*
and invites me in to lunch. I can't believe
she's become so like you, only more beautiful.
Me — beautiful? I hear your I'm-from-Missouri twang.

And yes you were —
that brown leanness and the austere hair pulled back
but mostly the crow eyes and the way you held me
with your talk when I came like a bird to your feeder.

So scorn me —
I'll return next time to Emily, who now
pares cheese, ladles soup and divides precisely
the last of the apple pie. If I squint
my left eye and look into shadow, she becomes
you, and when I visit in years to come I may forget
and call her by your name.

RETURN OF THE BLUE RUNNER

In those days your feet
tattooed pavement
beneath her window
rousing the dogs to song.
Catch as catch could
those travelling feet
Oh how you could go
Blue Runner.
But times change
feet lag, youth's
beat mocks us.

From this absurd distance
we learn you've taken
to water, swimming
in all weathers
sending wild spring
promises in winter.
You know how time
betrays all lovers
how no one waits
suspended forever.

Still, hearing of your
water prowess
she calendars off days
while you move this way
oh Blue Swimmer
to invade again
the heart's red estuaries.

TATTOOED MAN

— to Charles Salter, Jr., with appreciation

Each elbow is caught in a black spider web;
talons needled on the knuckles turn
his fists into leopard paws, and the spots
of that beast show through fake rents
    in his own hide.

His first tattoo was a cross —
at thirteen. Since then skulls
and demons and hell fire have eclipsed
    God's scaffolding.

A snake slithers down one arm
to perish in dragon fire.
A mother's heart pulses above his own
and a rose blooms on each breast.
A new picture appears with every change
of pose — and who knows what goes on
    below the waist?

Above the blood and brimstone,
the paisley skin and screaming flesh,
his head and neck emerge spared,
his face undeniably handsome.
Any lover could embrace him
but for this obsession with needling
garish colors into his body —
        no skin-deep thing.

OLD MAN REFUSING PROZAC

Don't they know it's just some sigh
of wind, some ghost voice whispering
to you *jump, jump* — off the tower
or bridge suspended over rapids?
A vision it is, sound as any foolish
cheerfulness. I just see deeper
is all; I know how love gets wiped
clean in one bad moment, one
wrong choice, one split second
of recklessness, when whatever
is out there steps in, takes
over. You're a goner for sure
without meaning any harm to any
soul, including yourself.

They make a big thing about my
losing my mama at birth, guilt
because she died for me, but
truth to tell it never would
have crossed my mind if they'd
not claimed it for me, hung
it round my neck. No, I never
gave it much thought. Pretty
thing she was in her summer
dress and cartwheel hat laughing
at my daddy — I guess my daddy —
aiming his Brownie camera
at her heart. Or could have been
some other man she loved first.

And why I never married was,
the only girl I loved married
elsewhere and who could blame
her — rich fellow and handsome
as they come. I wished her well
and let her go, refusing my ring
back. I've had my pleasures
here and there but it was clear
my luck would be losing first
choice in everything, just about,
and I could cast away love
and be that much better off.

Kids? Well, there's the rub
as Shakespeare said — yes,
I picked up him and the Bible
along the way but never got
religion or any sheepskin.

But I watch the stars and note
the seasons, and winter never
bothers me. I hole in like any
burrowing creature, then come
out in spring to see the bulbs
in glory, stand under the fruit
trees and the dogwood looking
like some fair woman's dream
of a tree in heaven. The redbud
is my favorite, bright ghost

among the pines, not quite enough
to wrap your eye around, surprising
you at every step. And so I go
through winter, spring, survive
the summer. And then there comes
the fall, when sometimes I keep my
balance but other times drop like
the leaves, welcoming the blessed
hibernation of my quilt-piled bed.

THE PRISONER WRITES THREE LETTERS

(1935)

1. To His Daughter

Don't you ever write me again, little Meg,
that I never loved your mama. I dream
of her there at the piano in that black
and silver dress, her black and silver
hair falling down her back. I can hear
the pure notes of her songs — "Corrina,
Corrina," "May I Sleep in Your Barn..."
and "Birmingham Jail" (and me today sitting
in a Carolina one just like it).

In those years before all the lies
and sorrows came, I could love her
all night, wake in the morning and love
her some more. Now that you know
what that kind of love is like,
let me tell you, little girl,
it was what made you and that's no lie.

So don't say, don't think —
your blue-eyed daddy didn't love
your black-eyed mama, and know this —
if she was here today she'd tell
you that same sure truth
that you would have to believe.

51

2. To His Brother-in-Law Junius

Brothers we were, Junie, before I ever married Margaret
— me and you fishing on Doe Creek — a memory I'll keep
to my dying day which may not be far off, 'cause when it
comes to life in this hell hole, give me death every time.
But to get back to what I was saying, Brothers we were,
no in-law to it.
               No in-law of mine — outlaw, outlaw!
you hollered at the trial and froze me with your coal-
                              hard eyes.
   Junie, I couldn't believe so much hate could live
in you. You know I never meant to harm her. At least read
these words I scratch on paper, writing by moon and prison
light. Here is how it happened —
                              I meant to get just him,
but the way they were tangled there on the bed, bedspread
my little mama crochetted thrown careless to the floor —
you could not tell where one's flesh ended and the other's
began. You know I've got a sure-fire aim, and I had him
                              dead in my sights.
   And then they moved, and what I thought was target
turned out to be her breast. As she fell away, there just for
a second, all I could think was, Now I got him -- and fired.
But the minute his head exploded, I rushed to her, praying
there was something there to save. Prayed aloud to the God
who's never there when you need Him.
                              Then I eased her down
to the floor — out of his blood. Blood on my hands, my

shirt, even in my eyes. Swimming in their blood, I was.

Like some madman I raced to the highway and hailed the first
car that came by. Young Dawson Epps was driving, that Epps
who used to come courting little Meg.

He thought it was me
was shot, wanted to take me to the hospital, but No, I said,
drop me by the sheriff's office.

So that's my story, Junie,
or leastwise all I've got to tell...

3. To His Pastor

Preacher, I want to thank you for all you've done —
your prayers, your visits, your solemn face even,
there when I needed someone to talk to besides Jesus.
You said to let you know how it's going for me —
        best I can say is, I ain't dead yet.

My lawyer, he says the Unwritten Law might could
save me, but knowing my luck, it won't cover
my case. There's something about me, Preacher,
that struts the rascal. I come in that courtroom,
the women eye me, the men they want to go
for my gizzard with their knives. Way I am,
        I guess, but meaning no harm to no one.

Here's some money, and if you can collect
some more to put a proper tombstone for her
with these words that just now came to me —
    Killed by the Husband Who Loved Her
then her dates, her 42 years on this earth

and maybe a Bible verse if you can think
of one that suits her life, her death —
my death, Preacher, cause I'm not gonna
appeal if I get the chair. A little time
to see my girl Meg if she'll come here.
Please remind her I never hated Margaret —
hated him, that Yankee playboy, but her I loved
and will until my dying day — a day that may
        well come before this year is out...

A SMALL HOUSE

That house of mine that burned
well over twenty years ago
comes back unbidden (I want
to put it out of mind)
and brings the smells
of mildew and Dial soap
mingling to make, strange
as it sounds, a heady
and memorable bouquet.

Sometimes I hear the floor
furnace roaring like hell's
meanest devil plotting to burn
us all in our beds — and feel
the sneak-thief cold poking
its finger through spaces
where window sills had
separated from frames.

Defects come back to let me know
it was not all paradise, that house —
little more than shack it was —
not something to hold against
the heart next to love, or name
a wandering grief *lost cottage*.

Still, on summer nights
after the boys were sleeping
in their shoe-box rooms
and I could sit on the green-
blinded porch and sip wine
while reading three sentences
without interruption, I'd hear
an eerie owl like the ghost
of some demented woman
shivering *who-who-who*.

And up at dawn, coffee mug
in hand, sprawled boys still
owing two more hours to Sleep
I would listen for the invisible
bird that *zee-zee-zee'd*
up the scale till its notes
rose beyond the range
of human ear and merged
with celestial music.

BIDING TIME

In her sleep she often hears
the harmonica breathings
of old trains, and time
holds her in its steady whine.
It is too early to die
but too late for love,
she sometimes thinks.

Out there on cement tundra
some old bear-husband
may be pawing his way to her
wanting his dinner, growling
out the grocery list,
but she yearns for a lean-
loined, white-haired man,
still fit, to take her
into his bed once more.

When she opens ancestral
trunks, she forgets
what she was searching for
and loses herself in water-
stain patterns and the smells
of lost perfumes mixed
with camphor and cedar.

Maybe she should get a cane
with a silver dog head
or the dog itself whining
to go out; or better still
a cat to give long stares
through windows, scorning
everything out there,
circling finally into
its cushion of sleep.

RELIABLE HEAT

Above wind soughs, branch
breaks, squirrel gutterals
I can hear that good old
working-man furnace
throbbing, throbbing...

like a steady husband
coming through snow
carrying beer and eggs
and a little country
treat like molasses...

Never lets you down
till he dies, plunged
headfirst into a snow bank —
and that's just how
I see this old furnace...

Big Furnaceman yells:
Better rip 'er out!
(lungs, thudding heart,
bone cracks), replace
with new unit two feet

by one and a quarter
computerized to serve you.
Listen, Big Furnace Man,

I know those models — they
sigh out with first frost.

Just light that pilot —
I'll stick with my faithful
good-husband furnace
that comes through for me
every winter night.

THE CAT AND THE BEAR

The orange and white cat
with lynx ears
watches me struggle
street wood up the back stairs
(old lumber from wrecked
houses that will burn
with eerie phosphorescence).
She is warm at her kitchen window
across the way. *What are you doing?*
her outraged stare asks.

Seeing me wrapped in my scrounging
costume (fake fur coat and hat),
she could take me for a bear.
Go away, creature, her eyes say.
I huff the wood up three steps,
then pause for breath. She moves
to get a better view. *That crazy
bear*, I hear her thinking,
what does it think it's doing?

Listen, cat — don't snub *me*!
You're an animal for life
I for only a brief while.
Tomorrow my furnace will kick
back on; next month spring may
creep up my stairs. Meanwhile
a woodsman lithe and running,

for all his crop of snow-white
hair, will bound up these stairs
with a load of fresh-cut cedar
logs and turn me into a queen.

From then on there will be only
decorative little fires to lend
charm to dinners for two. The bear
will hang in the closet, and I will
steal across the alley and kidnap you.
We will live happily ever after, we
three, you snoozing upon my hearth.

THOMAS FEEDS THE PIGEONS

They wait in their paisley dress
pink rubber feet gripping
squirrel-scarred limbs
eyes trained upon the door
from which Thomas will soon
emerge bearing a sand pail
of seed. "Birds!"
he will cry, granting them
equality with boys.

Since he was a baby
in a basket Thomas
has brothered with birds
watching with deep eyes
their wing shadows
hearing their calls.

What do you see, Thomas,
with your boy eyes?
What can you tell us
that our books
do not reveal?

THE COLOR GREEN

"Write my green name,"
he says, handing me
a peeled crayon.
And I write it —
green as glass
green as his
Christmas socks
green as the eyes
of the man who should
have lived to be
his godfather —
green, green, green.

Oh child, I will write
your green name
on all the trees —
each limb, each leaf
and on all tendril vines
I will inscribe
slim T's, full O's
sprawling M's
to make in green
your name again, again
for the world's neighborhood
to read: THOMAS

selections from...

FAMILY & OTHER STRANGERS

(Word Works, 1986)

BIBLIOPHILE

Because when it came, that fire,
I rejoiced that the boys all
got out alive, their scant scars
and even the dog that ran back
burnt offerings I could afford
to give the conflagration god.
And because I saw it as symbol
of that other fire I could not
put out and finally succumbed to —
the books of my father seemed
hardly worth the grieving.

But now, these ten years after,
I want them all back — notes
and interlinear glosses, spidered
marginalia, his cartoon of Mother
the day she bobbed her hair. I want
the leather bindings, marbled end
papers, uncut pages of obscure
editions holding their secrets fast,
want them with a child's fierce greed.

For each thing lost or burned
or thrown away too soon, I wrap
a tight fist around another —
the Indian head pennies my Uncle
George hoarded, the Mercury dimes
Anna his wife would sweeten

with Horn and Hardart sugar,
even the stamps bringing 1940
letters from Japan.

Lately I've placed the shoes
of the dead beside my door
let their hats hang in view till
I could bear to relinquish them
and in my sleep I learn to read
(before the fire takes them)
messages in a familiar hand.

MATRIX

Even at this moment I catch
my grandmother's preening
look — something close to
hauteur — as I pass the hall
mirror and settle a hat
over the forehead she willed me.
Sometimes my voice speaks
her sharp *Look out!*
to a street-darting child.

Then there's my mother
who inhabits my body too
fleetingly for me ever
to catch; still, there she is,
adored girlchild, propelled
in insouciant movements
to some additional seduction.

One could spend one's life
turning each femur and clavicle,
each vertebra, toward light to read
the matrix imprinted there.

POSING WITH A GREAT-GRANDMOTHER

(1932)

The lady photographer awaits the light —
we sit framed by flowering trees
Granny erect in her stiff chair
I leaning against her bones.
We know each other in small ways.
I devour her childhood —
how she learned to knit on stiff straws
made pins out of rose thorns
drank parched persimmon coffee.

One day she watched blue Yankees
march down a road embroidered
in forget-me-nots, through boxwood
past loom house, where silver
lay buried in piano boxes...

Always war has its games, its bag
of tricks, multiple disguises —
one day, re-entering a December
world out of the seasonless
Sunday matinee, I will hear
the name *Pearl Harbor* and see
down the pointing-finger street
townspeople frozen in stark
poses of disbelief...

When the light comes
the lady photographer
drapes Granny's shawl
arranges my stiff bangs
then goes behind her black-
draped tripod to fix us
together in time.

FAMILY ALBUMS

There is always a grandmother
sitting on the funeral chair
brought to the graveyard
or posed at the porch edge
where the light is good enough,
and one child — usually a tow
head — owls his neck around
to peer at her, making a blur.

There is the young wife in-law
mad at the husband who won't give
her babies, the patriarch with beard
to waist — sometimes there, often not:
He is not dead / He only sleepeth
his tombstone may read, inspiring
one young scholar to blurt out,
But they buried him anyway!

One bright Alice holds a cat
against her pinafore; and we see
over and over, the apron-stringed
mother holding her sailor-suited
son so he will never run away.
Boys growing up to kill the *Heinie*
or the *Jap* — in the cemetery we count
the tattered flags that mark each war.

Someone always writes on the back
of these pictures: *Mama in her last
year,* or *Nothing but kids and dogs
in the front row.* Here, though —
look through this magnifying glass
at the face of your mother, young
enough to be your grandchild now.

NEARING THE END

It is not just that her bones crack
like twigs a giant has stepped on
or that her gut sings in the long
twilight; there are other signs —
the presence of ghosts.

They bring their faces next to hers
wanting recognition. "Pshaw,"
she says, "I haven't time."
She is good at tamping down
the panic that rises when sun
pinks the road; often she lets in
stray cats to tick before the fire.

Back in her home town whenever
there was a funeral, a black man
in a top hat came to get signatures
in a white satin book.

Moving along the stations of her life
she recognizes the signs of dreams —
in a house of splendid rooms
she asks, Which one is mine?
Through a window she watches
a childhood friend prepare
a party; she has her invitation.

At night beneath her window
rough-hewn men confer.
They roll their wagons up
build their camp fires
wait...

MATRIARCH

The moment I took her from the box
I knew she was kin — high browed,
inscrutable eyed, composite
of my grandmother and her rival
sister, come together in this,
their grandmother's, face.

To a grandchild she would say,
"How bad you do need switching!"
Yet she swiftly defended
the falsely accused: "Annie
is a wild, *hoydenous* creature,
but she is a high-toned, honorable
child and would scorn to tell a lie."

"God catch it," she would cry
when a child stumbled toward fire,
and some divine representative
always did — white or black,
male or female, the rescue
was what mattered, wrought
by whatever hand.

She herself had just one — the left,
a broken arm set badly, sawed off
when she was sixteen. The surgeon
fell in love with her austere beauty,
died before he could claim her.
She wore a black cape to hide
the missing arm, pinned her handwork
to her skirt to hold it fast.

On her back, some spider hand
has lettered *Big Mother.*
I keep her stern visage
upon my memory's eye
holding it against a time
when I might need rescue
by the left hand of God.

VALEDICTORY

— for Caroline

Friends rise this Mother's Day
to harvest all the roses, bringing
them like bridal offerings.
The churchyard, despite an Irish rain,
seems more fit for wedding
than for funeral.

I want a country Baptist choir
to shout your name out loud
but this stern hymn, sung
"in unison/with spirit" must serve
and Church of England words
thy servant Caroline
daughter, wife, mother, friend
commit you to an ordered God.

I'm here, old friend, late but here,
fist wrapped around your last strong words —
"Most of the times were good."
And I grab them back, those times:
Dixie Inn chow mein
cribbed Latin, bicycle brigade
even backyard sandbox
when your green eyes
awesome even then
stared me out for friend.

We leave the churchyard
yet cannot quite relinquish you —
we need your clear mirror
to show us who we are
the sense our days make.
We have not pinched off enough
of your woman-wit
to service our own lives.

How can this house stand without you
to hold it in place? My hand
touches the acorn wallpaper,
the small lamp that burns the night.
I pry my fingers from your life
but still your body stirs the air
your voice forms from consonants
floating in the room. It takes
our collective wisdom not to keep watch
upon the stairs till you descend. Why
are you not here with us at this party?

Hold still, old dear — one last photo:
sharp bones, spare flesh, green eye
caught in merriment or warning,
now lie detector, now monitor of pain.
Let's capture the high-arched foot

extended in emphasis — rare vanity point —
the serviceable hands with their blunt nails
the fine and close-cropped hair.
Finally, we must record the voice
that fashions wit or wisdom
out of any scrap of talk.

We begin the celebration of your grace,
your gallantry; predict the sure working
of genes within your daughters: their voices
answering in your accents, their bodies
leaning to your measure. We must move on
to lesser rooms, clutching the words
there was not time to say.

EMERGENCY ROOM

The plastic mask they place
over my mother's face
clouds with her breath
clears with her non-breath
the half-moon eyes
like my grandmother's
that last day's dying.
"She is failing," I tell them;
still, they drink their coffee.

The mask makes me think
of Halloween —
costumes she made me
sitting up all night
rattling the old Singer
the way she rattled
the red Essex
over purple dirt roads.

Behind the mask I hear
a faint child-mew
like the sound I made
that time they thought
I was dying and she held
the Japanese parasol
over me in the dark
never able to slip away
without my crying out,

"Put that umbrella back up."

She has a message —
one word...important.
Warning? Farewell?
What must she tell this child
of hers, offspring of Eros
and Thanatos? I lean close —
"Hello," she says. The mask
clouds, then clears:
again, "Hello."

Hello, my mother, hello.

DREAM OF A FATHER

Last night for the first time
I dreamed of you. Though still tall
you had at last grown old
your feet failing to grip ground
a cane in one hand, the other
resting hard upon the hood
of that black Pontiac —
the one Mother and I drove
over corrugated roads
filling its vases
with wild flowers.

Once as I lay tantrum-strewn
on the back seat, she cried
"I cannot stand it any more."
What? Life? Me — a poor
exchange for you?

In this dream (like a snapshot
gradually set in motion)
you moved slowly toward the door
I held open. You said,
"Well, let's go." Where?
You did not tell me.
I awoke before you got in.

IT IS HERE...

...the time when
the cock crows and the wind
stirs and the maple makes
no imprint on the far wall
and here in this room
is the familiar wheat
smell of a man.

...a year to weep
for mothers and lovers
to place wreaths
on graves and bring the stone
that says three strong times
I release you.

...a day to cover the ears
against the ghost that whispers
close to the breastbone
I will never   I will never
　　I will never...

...an hour when we
avoid the rat running
at the eye's edge
and stifle voices
not our own, yet not
quite those of ancestors...

...a moment to think
of my uncle, scribbling
the world's news
on a penny postcard

...a second to see
my grandmother holding
am amber of caramel
up to the light
to test its purity.

OLD DURHAM

"Don't take your eyes off this road for one second
or you're dead" — an uncle voice sounds
upon my ear drum and I'm back learning to drive
on Old Durham ... Dead Man's Curve
where thirty-two species of roses lure you
— if you are not warned —
into an eternity of poppies.

Don't look at those iris   Don't look at those lilies
Ease your foot off the gas   Don't put that brake on hard
Now just go slow and ride with the curve...

Past MacFarling's Store plastered with Tube Rose Snuff
and Teaberry Gum   past the bootlegger's brick house
built with moonshine whiskey   past hanging portulaca
and tire swings roped to chinaberry trees...

Ragweed children wave from pine-slick porches
as though they expect a train engineer
to lean hugely from his cab and spread
a mammoth hand in benediction.

WARNING IN THE MOTHER TONGUE

He may not kill you right away
or use a gun to do it. He could
live with you twenty years
then turn you out in the woods
or run you down on the highway
driving off in that car
the color of winter apples.

The men with the light-tan eyes
and mill hair are the worst —
the ones who know how to turn
you against yourself. A girl
your age needs to listen
to a wiser voice. So ask —
that is, if he allows you time.

UNCLE WILLIAM, AUNT MARY

He kept a loaded gun between them in the bed
to shoot her phantom lovers. Sometimes he saw
her walk barefoot across snow to reach them;
her calm voice beside him, *William, William,*
did not change that certainty. Crazy,
some said, gone on laudanum, said others.
A son, teller in the bank, struck by lightning,
three girls lost in one typhoid summer — enough
to do it even if he'd been sane to start with.
She'd married, they said, to keep from teaching
but that did not explain her staying with him.
When he died she wrote her niece, He looked
so handsome when we laid him out — his blue
suit like one he'd worn when he came courting.

MAGGIE

After her husband's long dying
she wanted to become a nurse
but her six grown children said

> *Mama, what will people*
> *You'd wear yourself*
> *You wouldn't last a*
> *Besides we all*

She listened to them
said a weary *all right.*
Still, there was the way
she draped a shawl across your legs
when you lay sprawled on a couch
the way she rubbed your head
with glycerin and rose water...

FOUR BAG LADIES

1.

She rushes at me, as to a cab,
explains she was lying
in an open window
forgetting it was not spring
that she was no longer young
and for this indiscretion
is being cruelly punished
by a bout with her hip.
Will I take her to the doctor?
Upon the hood of my car
she places her shopping bag
from which the face
of a silent screen star pouts.

She is the same tamoshantered
woman who sings the Marseillaise
at midnight Metro stops
inviting strolling sailors
to join in. Her green eyes
have become milky agates
with age — age that cannot
alter the structure of that face.
"Of course," I say, but she
has already got in, settling
the movie queen beside her.

2.

At the Hilton a black-garbed cripple
propels herself by ancient cane
through the lobby, asking the way out.
Several teeth are missing, yet beauty
lingers in this no-longer-hospitable
mansion. I lead her through
the coffee shop, where briefly
we enjoy the illusion of summer —
hanging baskets, fake bird song,
wax fruit, abundant chintz —
then into fall air. Her mouth
accommodates a smile. She promenades
her moth-balled regalness —
still there, even with missing
teeth, game leg, tumor
of shopping bag.

3.

My mother gets off the bus at East Capitol
carrying one shopping bag marked UNPACK.
A second, smaller one features a pyramid
of smiling cats. The first bag holds
a muskrat coat she'd hoped a Hong Kong

tailor from India could use to line
a black cashmere. The tailor was baffled
by her Southern accent, she by his pseudo-
British speech ("'Tis prepossible!")
The deal was off.

Not so long ago she could have done
the job herself, just like her mother
before her, and hers before her
and even hers before her, one-armed
though she was — all rendering costume
miracles from scraps and trim.

"Now I shall go to the li-berry,"
my mother says, satirizing the speech
of her mountain town, circa 1902.
From her Library of Congress shelf
she takes down the last of C.P. Snow,
reads till almost dark, then goes
to let the guard inspect the pyramid
of smiling cats, search the bags
for incunabula and wave her on.

4.

Just yesterday, a day
I felt quite fondly young,
my second son called to say

he'd never put me in a nursing home;
instead, he'd put me (pause)
in the basement of his home
(still to be built)
and he and his wife
(still to be married)
would look after me.
The next day my first son called
to say that quite good buys
could be had in California
and money could be arranged.

Thanks, both of you, but no,
and no again — I must be
my own wood carrier ... (I hear
my mother keening: the street wood
I pick up will asphyxiate me
as it burns, its nails produce
lockjaw; the abandoned books
I collect in my rucksack have been
fondled by tubercular hands) ...

Yes, I must be my own fire tender,
wood carrier, hearth sweeper —
wear out, not rust out, as my old
nurse used to say, when at 88
she painted her black iron flower
pots a screaming blue.

FACTS OF LIFE

Our gang, half boys, half girls
first learned the word
from a dirty joke
whose punch line was
"Mama and Daddy are upstairs fucking."

Slowly shedding innocence
we imagined our parents
heroically readying themselves
for the annual act of procreation.

Did they ever hold each other —
these old turtles, these de-clawed pussy cats,
who now argue daily over the proper brand
of breakfast tea, how best to wind the clock?

Ah yes! In old pictures we can see
a shine to their faces — a secret pleasure
they must have had, planting us,
and later the siblings we begged for.

MY SONS DISGUISED

I see you as Pilgrims
full of turkey and self importance,
as red kangaroos
chasing a pink rabbit
in the church basement.

Raccoons, fat cats, sleazy comics,
playing cards (jack and joker),
monsters, minute men —
everything but girls.

But this year's costumes
are your most complete disguises:
six foot two with beards
and bass voices, boots
that stretch halfway
across the kitchen.

My neck aches from looking up
and my head throbs
where your palms have
tapped out condescending
messages of affection.

CONVERSATION WITH A SON

He brings me seasoned wood
on winter's coldest day
and builds a teepee fire

If I were Choctaw
and you Squaw Mother
we couldn't talk like this —
you know, the manhood thing.

Then how ... I want to know.

I'd talk to the fire
and you would overhear.

The fire he built burns on
long after he has gone.
I bend to catch his words
pulsing within those flames.

SLAVE DAUGHTER

She entered the best back doors
in town — bread-kneader
translator for owls and babies
interpreter of myths, goddess
of mint beds and sunflowers.

Arbiter, healer, diplomat,
she earned her five dollars.
In memoriam I climb
her high abandoned stairs
and knock at her back door.

LATE MAY

Today I sit on my porch and wait for magnolias
to unfold brown petals that whiten in new light
the pulse before love's climax, the pre-birth hush...

In the country room, from the grandfather bed
with its altar headboard and candle shelves
we heard the bees ping our window
after they took the nectar of each magnolia.
What mad honey they made of those blossoms!

In this new place, I await a second blooming
and feel a quickening — promise of Sarah-birth —
giving me this poem which now I send to you.

SELLING THE HOUSE

I know this house
better than my own body —
the rounded newel post
like the head of a child
Dummkopf to the touch,
the whispers in attic beams
cries of hinges, chimney sighs.

We have peeled down the rooms
to our first hopes
when walls sprang smooth
from their wallpaper shrouds.

Light reclaims corners
and foreign sounds travel
floorboards. Stored notes
tremble and I hear
the timbre of gone voices.

In the crepe myrtle
that has shaped itself to *S*
a mockingbird reviews its songs.
I open my rib cage
and set its cousin free.

BURNING THE JOURNALS

In the event
of my death
Destroy totally

Yet you know no one will
so you burn them
but as the curling sheets
reveal a name, you reach
for the crimsoning paper
that shudders into ash
even as your hand
touches its heat.

1.

Here at December's start
comes the desperation of spring
spring with black tree bones
against a mid-May sky.
At night the turn begins
and by morning trash cans
roll through alleyways like drums.
Forgotten wind chimes
play a winter music.
Dogs mutter and curse
in their kennels.

My son's friend Jacob
murdered in Pennsylvania
beaten to death, then
run over with a car —
in his fist, a handful
of woman-hair.

Buried in a vault
coffin shoved into a slot
name, scant dates
on a brass plaque.

Going to pay his respects
my son wants to shout
Hey Jake, whatcha doin'
in there? Get out,
man, get out.

It's harder, he says,
to be the living
than to be the dead.

My friends begin to die —
explosion of cells
lunar eclipse in the brain's
silent half — I see myself
the one Custer raider spared,
lone tree in a ruined forest.

2.

April — and we return to fires,
burn the last of winter's wood:
wainscoating from old houses,
mud-clotted tree branch and root.
At seven the sun returns —
a double rainbow divides the sky
one half churned gray
one half pure blue
like our lives, like our lives.
Burned down, the fire pulses
with orange light, breathes upward,
not quite meeting with wood.

In the dream they said
He's been here...just left...
looking for you. I ran
into the street calling.
Ahead I saw his beret.

But as I chased him
every man, then every youth
then every male child
all wore his beret.

Everywhere, everywhere
(I could not tell him

from all the boys and men)
a brotherhood of berets.

Sometimes even now I long for it
that house of mine singing on its hill —
the sly land slope, fireflies rising
from earth like sparks the land
sends up. I hear the ghost-owl
whisper and the mid-morning bird
zee zee zee up the scale
beyond the range of human ear.

Gone now.
Who sang the dirge?
Is there some note in ether
some shape sketched on air
some stone?

3.

We sat on her porch, looked
at the mackerel patches of lake
through pines, rocked in the chairs
of childhood, laughed in almost
the old way. She said,
"Sin becomes you —
it shows in your face."

When I told her I dreamed
of boxes, she warned,
"Be sure one of them
is not satin lined."

We watched the gyrations
of a moth, orange lion's head
imposed on its dull dun body.
"A mating dance," I ventured.
"A dance of death" —
her level green eyes
stared me down. We watched
it make circular,
ritual flutterings,
then fold its wings
to stillness.

How long should one inhabit
the houses of the dead?
After you hang their herbs
and piece together the bowls
of their making, should you
shut the door behind you,
leave the key in its hiding place?

It is not that I fear I will be next —
rather, that all will leave me,
a child not invited to the party.

I dream of them, my dead:
Last night they sat around a table,
some scarred, some with heads
like ruined planets, others
scaled down to bone.

This is how we are now
they seemed to say.
They saw me, beckoned —
join us, join us.
How kind they are, I thought,
they want me still.

Yet I turned and went back through the door
I had entered. They resumed their conversation,
not so much forgetting as allowing me to leave.

4.

Even though it is Thanksgiving day
the school bell rings next door
marking the exits and entrances
of ghost children.
In this false spring
a cherry tree blooms
at the playground's edge

and down the road
a horse with sycamore markings
comes to the fence to share
its stillness with me.

"There are still many good things
left for us to do," he says,
so today we visit the Cathedral.
He is content to sit first
in the gazebo, then in the close
studying flying buttresses,
rose windows...

He is paled and subtly thinned
but his hands hold their power.
He poses for pictures
with a certain pride,
a knowledge of his own beauty
that is not vanity.

Later he tells me,
"I do not know this body now."
Continents collide, explode;
the body universe
cannot survive its war.

"Do you ever want to cry?" I ask.
"All the time," he says.

"But you cannot?"
He shakes his head.
"Then I will cry for you.
Every afternoon at four o'clock
I will come and cry for you."

When I give him the last pictures
he studies the Old Master look
of the river, then the planes
of his own face. "You would
have to see me from many angles
to know who I am," he says.
That last day I showed him
his mother's face
read the sonnet he asked for
("How like a winter...")
held a narcissus bloom
for him to smell the forced perfume.
To all these gifts, he said,
Remarkable, remarkable,
keeping before him the wonder
the wonder of this world
though death greened his face.

When I left he called my name
three strong times.
I remember my return
but a veil falls over the rest —

what he said, why he called.
Perhaps his calling is what matters.

These bones he has become
will grow into a tree
not yet yellowed
in its sere, or turn
into a running boy
chasing or escaping
one cannot tell.
But rise they must
and rise they will.

Meantime I stay beside this door
where geraniums left to wither
give pungence to winter's air
and listen for the gate-click
count out the six-year gift
each time more slowly, to make
it last until he becomes a tree
a running boy returned.

selections from...

BURNSITE

(Washington Writers' Publishing House, 1979)

BURNSITE

Even with siftings of rain
the fire held its coals
for three days
gnawing down to stone.

Now we must decide
whether to resurrect
or abandon — let all
fall into timelessness.

Shall we leave shards?
topple chimney stones?
let tree shade stripe
the empty yard?

A plane whines;
in deep woods an owl
barks. Beyond that,
a dog sobs like a man.

Around us cicadas tick
like timepieces hidden
in grass. Our answers
balance in the sound.

INVADER

God what a wind!
Rapist on the prowl   he slams his fist
against the pane   shatters ice like glass
slides open the unlocked latch
thrusts one leg over the sill
Quick! I slam the window shut   click the lock
        how he howls!

I will escape him through the back alleys of sleep
but that monster wind has knocked me up with nightmares
        and I wake to find him   beast that he is
hanging by his paw hands from my window ledge
        whispering obscenities.

THE OLD WOMEN

First they stop speaking,
even the voluble ones,
the reminiscent ones.
Sometimes they dye their hair
a strange orange, a gaudy blue.
They no longer look at people
but stare hard into the faces
of cats, of sunflowers.
They lose keys, names,
finally themselves,
spooling down to the last inch
of tight-wound thread.

KISMET

That old woman
her head heavy
as a seeded sunflower —
why do I keep meeting *her*
as I rush down cement track?

Why listen for her tapping
as she surmounts the stairs
bringing both feet to each step
while below the chicken claw
of her hand the iron railing
stretches like a railroad link
toward me?

MATRIARCH IN MORNING

She wakes. Hands stray
to belly swelled as in one
last late pregnancy.
Bird chorus terrifying
grief wailing through her
like winds.

Sons and brothers
kinsmen of the hills
lost in terrible moments
of fire and water. They call
needing her still.

Downstairs, closing his blinds,
her surviving son prepares for bed.
At twilight he will rise,
ring his insistent bell.
Her spine aches from his call.

In the next bed
her mother surprises her
with lusty snores —
one who lives in the interstices
of old time, still beautiful
with her meringue of hair.

And in the small room
where marionettes

dangle from ceiling
her daughter's child lies.
In her own flesh
she feels this girl
make one last turn
into the coil of sleep
before awakening.

THE LOST CHILDREN

Why did the picture album
always open at the black pages
of coffined children, hands
steepled over lilies?

Who were they, these boys
who left their nicknames
and playthings behind?
These girls, whose hair
was framed in shadow boxes?

Were these the same ones
who in earlier pages
twirled hoops, rode
goat carts, posed
in moon-shaped hats,
bull dogs named
Big Boy and Pretty Face
glued to their thighs?

And who came to photograph
the chiseled epitaphs
leaving their shadows
on miniature gravestones?

QUICK-SKETCH OF A GREAT-GRANDMOTHER

(1854-1946)

Crane-graceful
hair parted in middle
ears bent slightly out
feet in mouse slippers
dress to ankles
my great-grandmother sits
in the pachyderm maroon
Montgomery Ward rocker

tatting   writing her children
rocking the cat   knitting Afghan squares
shelling peas   playing solitaire
     memorizing the kings of France

each thing in its proper time-slot.

She wears a cotton glove
to stroke the cat;
her feet dance in place
to the music of Phil Spitalny
and his all-girl orchestra.
When Kaltenborn speaks,
she listens gravely,
remembering other wars.
At 3.30 every afternoon
she drinks half a glass

of Coca-Cola prescribed
by an indulgent physician

Men prefer her to Whistler's version
and make pilgrimages to bring

crystallized fruit   laced hankerchiefs
spider-webbed shawls   gentle wines
    pictures of their mothers

On chosen days she rises
goes into the kitchen to make
Sally Lunn for our supper.
Those evenings we eat nothing
but that melting bread-cake
with acorns of butter. Afterwards
she washes up the plates.

NIGHT PLACE

In barlight the knuckled men
move dominoes in silent games
words shudder on their lips
                    unsounded.
Here women are not wanted —
the clatter of their bracelets
                    distracts.

To be welcome you must be
either male or silent
as the mounted animals —
a bobcat grinning
at an eagle stretched
in dusty flight
the deer above the mirror
each of its feet nailed
at a rainbowed corner.

Go now — study your own face
framed within this massacre.

THE SON

I think of my grandmother
in the sealskin coat and toque made of rosepoint
journeying to the mountain that wrapped her dead
reading letters iced on stone, scant span of manhood:
                    Alexander
          September 18, 1899 — November 6, 1920
He had never known a woman.

Where did she hide her grief?
Did it tremble
in the never-still hands?
One day she ran an icepick
through her hand at dawn
and kept it hidden until dusk.

Just so, she kept her grief hard hidden
until her 95th year, when in the stare of her days
she mourned him in his broken beauty.
"Fifty years," I reminded her, "fifty years."

"So long a time!" she marvelled.
Then, almost in relief:
"So now there is nothing left
for me to do," and returned
to her hard-won peace.

RESURRECTION

An ordinary one takes longer
than the three-day miracle
but wait — it will come.
There must be time to cancel
the memory of oven doors
closing with soft pneumatic
whoosh, and artificial wreaths
fade slowly.

Then there are possessions —
soft hats resembling
their owners and sweater
pockets still bulging
with illegible notes.

But after six months or a year
at most, there begins
the benign haunting —
familiar hum or whistle,
brush upon clothing, upon skin;
presence, remembrance. You stand
at wintered windows and catch
their images in your face
their gestures in your limbs
spirits reclothing themselves
in your flesh.

INHERITANCE

Grandmother, all year
you've moved inside my skin
trained me to your ways
taken over lesser clay —
kinship claiming its own.

Yesterday in a junk-shop window
I became your glassed twin —
even to the brave coat
rescued from a son's discarding.

And my hand, become your own,
moved like a divining rod
toward the one true piece
of gold — I watched you
finger it through glass.

LEAVING HOME

Car loaded
one sock
locked in the door.
How can he see out
with all those clothes?
Couldn't he wait
and go tonight?
An owl's eyes he's got
better in dark.

I stand in morning's
skim milk light
seeing the diamonding
of latched gate
the rescued dog
street siblings
shoe-boxed pigeon.
Him, him, him —
too many snapshots!

We've said goodbye
it does not bear repeating.
The starter giggles into catch —
Wait! One more thing...
But he (hearing, not hearing)
drives on. Better anyway:
hard to pick one final thing
— warning, blessing —
and make it last
a lifetime.

PERSPECTIVE

This time our one window affords a stingy view:
Through spindled trees of winter we can see
chimneys with mortar triumphing over stone,
roofs of sky-matched tin; curtainless windows
opening into sun-missed rooms with tatters of roses.

Yet our window faces east. Wash it in rain water,
swing plants in its light. Meanwhile stare hard
into this rectangle of new morning;
fix shapes upon the memory's eyeball,
then close your eyes and let the forms return
as lost spires, spines of old dreams.

CITY WINDOW

Over what ether do they come
these country sounds
travelling to the boxes
we inhabit now?

Mourning dove and wood thrush
could be migration's strays
but explain if you can
cow bells and the laughter
of children born in 1925.

On any good day
we can hear second cousins
singing in their talk
and the home-town power plant
throbs in this city's pulse.

We sit among the macrame
of translated geraniums
our backs to Nazi buildings
prisons of greened light
and hear over invisible hills
the voices of grandmothers
calling us in from play.

AFTER THE FIRE

You say we need to walk the land again.
Why? comes my quick question —
let it all sleep, I say. *Come on,*
you insist, leading the way downhill.

The woods reclaim the road
blurring its contours. We ghost-walk
past white pine, pin oaks
with their rusted hammock hooks
boxwood with its fox smell
then take the brick path leading
nowhere now. Birds thrush up
and some child-cry sounds in woods
to bounce against the breast bone —
Crazy bird! singing past the phoenix time.

Let's leave these charred ruins
as playground for blue-tailed lizards
and the ghost of the gray cat
who watched them, extending
a paw, surprising herself with capture.
Should we mourn the 4 o'clocks
at the back door (or where
the back door was?) Weep for boys
who used to pry them open at noon?

(Thank God those boys
making hose rivers
for pirate boats
their naked bodies
Picassoed by shade
are memory phantoms
and not real ghosts.)

You are cheerful now
having found mendable items
which we pack in my rucksack.
Tomorrow we may throw them all out
but now they make a good weight
to take uphill. Where the road
starts its slow rise, we turn...
How tall the chimney looks
how long its shadow
without the house.